Cognitive-Behavioral Therapy

Cognitive-Behavioral Therapy

poetry by Tao Lin

MELVILLEHOUSE

BROOKLYN, NEW YORK

Melville House Publishing
145 Plymouth Street
Brooklyn, NY 11201

www.mhpbooks.com

Book Design: Kelly Blair

First Melville House Printing: May 2008

Library of Congress Cataloging-in-Publication Data
Lin, Tao, 1983-
  Cognitive-behavioral therapy / Tao Lin.
    p. cm.
  Poems.
  ISBN 978-1-933633-48-0
  I. Title.
  PS3612.I517C64 2008
  811'.6--dc22

                          2008007085

Printed in Canada.

3.

4.

1.

i will learn how to love a person and then i will teach you and then we will know

seen from a great enough distance i cannot be seen
i feel this as an extremely distinct sensation
of feeling like shit; the effect of small children
is that they use declarative sentences and then look at your face
with an expression that says, 'you will never do enough
for the people you love'; i can feel the universe expanding
and it feels like no one is trying hard enough
the effect of this is an extremely shitty sensation
of being the only person alive; i have been alone for a very long
    time
it will take an extreme person to make me feel less alone
the effect of being alone for a very long time
is that i have been thinking very hard and learning about
    existence, mortality
loneliness, people, society, and love; i am afraid
that i am not learning fast enough; i can feel the universe
    expanding
and it feels like no one has ever tried hard enough; when i cried in
    your room
it was the effect of an extremely distinct sensation that 'i am the

only person
alive,' 'i have not learned enough,' and 'i can feel the universe
expanding and making things be further apart
and it feels like a declarative sentence
whose message is that we must try harder'

today is tuesday; email me on saturday

the secret of life is decisiveness

and to describe something

i see the distance and move immediately into it

now i am really alone

from here i know these things: that a hamster is a lonely fist

that my poems exist to dispel irrational angers, that i want to hold
   your face

with my face

like a hand

the secret of life is that i miss you, and this describes life

tonight my heart feels shiny and calm as a soft wet star

i describe it from a distance, then move quickly away

i looked away from the computer with a slight feeling
of out-of-control anger; i saw you wearing a coffee-colored star-suit
there was a barely perceptible feeling on my face
that i was being crushed by the shit of the world
then i saw beyond the window to the tree, the house, and the street
the house and the street made mysterious binary noises
that negatively affected the tree's immense happiness
i observed this neutrally, without falling out of my chair

energy drinks help me achieve worldviews that allow me to forgive you
masturbation is underrepresented
in my poetry, it's a scientific fact
that our thoughts cause our feelings and behaviors
and there is a tingly sensation on the surface of my face
that feels like the binary nature of the universe
i feel severely confused and unable to function, i'll be right back
something behind my forehead is trying to crush my 'good feelings
    toward you'

.

my favorite emotions include 'brief calmness
in good weather' and 'i am the only person alive'
without constant reassurance i feel terribly lonely and insane
i have moved beyond meaninglessness, far beyond meaninglessness
to something positive, life-affirming, and potentially best-selling
i have channeled most of my anger into creating and sustaining an
    'angry face'
i have picked up a medium-size glass of coffee
and used it in the conventional way
because i am conventional in all situations, i'll be right back

the correct arrangement of words will make these bad feelings go away
     tonight
the incorrect arrangement of words will also make these bad feelings
     go away
tonight, because of the placebo effect, which always works
do we really live in an insane world of terrible loneliness?
i feel intense, uncontrollable eyebrows on my face
and something behind my forehead is making squishy noises
i should not allow an energy drink to affect my worldview
i enjoy a quiet night masturbating in front of the computer
with or without high speed internet
i'll be right back

my favorite situations include 'people doing what they say'
'people thinking factually,' and 'people crying alone in bed'
i don't know how to fix this mini-disc player
without a meaningful philosophy of life
i feel severely unable to move as fast as they do in martial arts movies
strong feelings of achievement later become barely perceptible
feelings of immense helplessness; i moved my body outside your house
past seven other houses
to meet you at the bus stop

2.

through repeated attempts at something impossible we will achieve
    'intense eyebrows'
'able to fall asleep faster at night' and 'is accepting human dishonesty,
    unreliability
and superstition the same as accepting death
limited-time, and the mysteries of being and existence?'
an out-of-control placebo effect rips a tree out of the ground
then immediately plants it back to avoid social situations
i told you i never get angry, only sad, i'll be right back
i am thinking of something shiny and round

and it is swinging around in the air

i feel most out-of-control when sitting quietly

with a blank face not thinking anything

then i leave the house with a mysterious feeling of having ruined both
    our lives

from the street i looked unreliable, sex-depraved, and 'is never not
    angry or sad'

this morning i sprayed sour apple lollipop perfume on the crotch of
    my pants

now i have to go do something to my penis

the indifference of the universe is an expansive shithead
with mysterious healing powers, a flat panel monitor, and a light blue
glow
i have talked too much shit about human beings to go outside
my heart feels like a medium-erect penis wrapped in saran wrap
until a ball of medium-erect penis
it is saturday, july 8th, 2006, 12:37 a.m.
i am lying facedown on my bed
through classical conditioning i have learned english and math

as a teenager i experienced existential despair as an unsexy sensation
of repressed orgasm in the chest; today i experience existential despair
as a distinct sensation of wanting to lecture you
on how i am better than you, without crushing your hopes and dreams
if this is about to become a social situation i will be right back
my unit of communication is the 200-page novel
always remember that i am better than you, according to me
small feelings of permanence later get wrapped and sold on amazon

sometimes with free shipping, negative thought patterns
immense helplessness, and the unidirectional force of binary powers
and powerful bestsellers; i feel exactly like an energy drink right now
irrational behavior is a temporary solution to a temporary problem
and a temporary solution to a temporary problem is a permanent
    solution
gradually an inspirational sentence appeared on the computer screen
i highlighted the sentence and pushed the delete button

and closed the file and looked out the window
through classical conditioning i have
learned to feel angry in all situations
i know exactly how to fix this relationship
through classical conditioning i know everything
my face feels slightly crushed by immense shit
the rest of myself feels like a rare form of the placebo effect
i have moved beyond saturday, july 8th, 2006, 12:37 a.m.
to friday, september 15th, 2006, 10:53 a.m.
i have to go do something, i'll be right back

that was bad; i shouldn't have done that

to prevent you from entering a catatonic state
i am going to maintain a calm facial expression
with crinkly eyes and an overall friendly demeanor
i believe in a human being that is not upset
i believe if you are working i should not be insane
or upset—why am i ever insane or upset and not working?
i vacuumed the entire house this morning
i cleaned the kitchen and the computer room
and i made you a meat helmet with computer paper
the opportunity for change exists in each moment, all moments are
    alone
and separate from other moments, and there are a limited number of
    moments
and the idea of change is a delusion of positive or negative thinking
your hands are covering your face
and your body moves like a statue
when i try to manipulate an appendage
if i could just get you to cry tears of joy one more time

are you okay?

i don't think telling someone 'don't feel sad' will console them

you need to do whatever you can to make them feel better

whenever your actions make them feel sad

and not stop until they feel better

read my text message and think about it

you just never seem happy with me anymore

even if i make you laugh

i think the damage i've done has become irreversible

i'm surrounded by endless shit

i can't move

where are you

  i just had a dream where i came to nyc but i didn't tell you and i took
    the subway

to your apartment and waited for your roommate to come out so i
    could sneak in

then i went into your room and crawled under your sheets from the
    end of your bed

and crawled to your face and kissed you then pet and hugged you

and we fell asleep

happy birthday

i drew you an ugly fish comic

will you visit me today?

i want to hold you

and kiss your face

i miss walking with you at night

In its room the hamster stared at a book by an author who had died. 'What if I died?' the hamster thought a little confused. The hamster had not yet met its hamster friend. The hamster was alone. It was an urban variety of an uncommon species of vegan hamster. Its room was small.

It had stacks of stolen books. The hamster had organic green tea extract that was stolen.

The hamster's toothpaste was stolen and it used stolen flaxseed lemon soap on its hair, which it cut itself. The hamster had an eleven-dollar toothbrush.

The toothbrush was stolen. The hamster was a recent college graduate. Some days it felt terrible, then realized while walking that it didn't feel terrible, but very good, and then felt relieved and consoled for the rest of the day until it went to sleep, though most other days after a few hours everything outside its head became a single unit of experience that entered its head—which was also its body—and then included its head, creating a single mass the hamster carried home and laid on a pillow.

The hamster's pillow was made of goose feathers. The hamster had found it in the refuge room.

The hamster's philosophy of life included rather than was dictated by veganism. If the hamster saw cheese or meat in the garbage it would process its choices—to eat or not eat—and in most circumstances eat the cheese or meat, so that later on it would not require as many resources to continue to exist and so could spend more money on things that would contribute to increasing the life-span of other organisms while also reducing pain and suffering in the world.

The hamster conceived this philosophy by observing that it did not commit suicide. 'I am perpetuating a conscious state of being by eating and breathing and thinking and not slitting my wrists,' the hamster thought unexcitedly, 'therefore my philosophy—derived from my actions, which are pre-philosophical, or something—is that I am a conscious being and I want to live, that all conscious beings not working towards or in the act of suicide also want to live, and that I should therefore behave in a way that allows the most organisms the most life.'

The hamster sometimes thought about war, politics, globalization, and world trade but mostly about things like death, writing, existence, loneliness, and meaninglessness that to it often preempted—despite its philosophy regarding the value of life—economy, capitalism, society, and materialism. The hamster lived in Manhattan. Later it moved to Florida; then, to be near its hamster friend, Pennsylvania. It had read over three hundred books of literary fiction, including almost all of Jean Rhys, Lydia Davis, Joy Williams, Lorrie Moore, Frederick Barthelme, and Richard Yates.

One night the hamster read a book that said HIV probably wasn't the cause of AIDS. The hamster told three other hamsters that HIV probably wasn't the cause of AIDS and two of the hamsters got angry at it.

An angry hamster looks exactly like an unangry hamster because the anger is within.

The hamster was unemployed. It stole from Whole Foods and other grocery stores and Virgin Megastore.

Each day the hamster walked in stores, put items in a black duffel bag, walked out of stores, and ate the items walking around. If the items were books it didn't eat them. It read them, sold them to used bookstores, or mailed them to hamsters it knew from the internet. The hamster eventually consumed, sold on eBay, or gave away over $8,000 worth of stolen goods. It said to another hamster, 'You have to be retarded to be caught stealing.' Later the hamster was caught stealing and banned for life from Whole Foods. The hamster stole only from publicly-traded companies.

The function of a publicly-traded company is to increase its worth so that stockholders will have more money now than before. A publicly-traded company must increase profits or convince the hamster population that profits will increase soon or else it will exist less, then not exist.

When one publicly-traded company loses business another publicly-traded company gains business, except when an independently-owned company gains the business.

An independently-owned company is not existentially required to increase profits but can use profits to increase wages, improve quality, lower prices, fund charities, or institute money-losing but socially-beneficial programs as ends in themselves rather than means for increasing profits.

Outside a 24-hour grocery store a homeless hamster lied to the hamster four times, each time gaining twenty to thirty dollars.

After the second lie the hamster said, 'Are you lying to me?' The homeless hamster said it was not. The homeless hamster talked about Christianity. The hamster listened politely and gave the homeless hamster twenty dollars and the homeless hamster danced into an alleyway, becoming smaller as it got further away from the hamster, who liked what was happening, partly because the dance was a jig.

The third lie the homeless hamster said to the hamster was that it had a kidney infection from eating out of the trash. It said it pissed blood. 'What happened?' the hamster said, and stared at the homeless hamster. The homeless hamster was silent. The homeless hamster said it was cured. It said they put a needle into its kidney and took out the poison, and that it needed money to have residence for one week, so that it could get a job.

The homeless hamster moved very fast the fourth time and said it had eight years training of a kind of martial arts. The hamster nodded. The homeless hamster very quickly turned away from the hamster then turned back suddenly with a face that displayed no discernible emotion and no discernible lack of emotion.

The hamster was impressed a little and thought briefly about how it was very well nourished and ate mostly only organic foods but felt like it could not move nearly as fast as the homeless hamster just did.

'You look strong,' the hamster said.

There was another homeless hamster the hamster had given a dollar to, about two minutes earlier, and the homeless hamster with martial arts said, 'Do you want me to jump him?' The hamster said not to jump the other homeless hamster, who had a beard.

The bearded hamster was very large and round and stood about thirty-feet away. It wore a large black trench coat and had a facial expression like it just woke from twelve hours of sleep and didn't know where it was. The hamster had seen the homeless hamster with the beard many times before and it always had that expression.

the power of ethical reasoning

the most callous, stupid things were done
just because regulations required them
and no one thought to change the regulations
there are many human beings locked away
in special wards throughout the country
some of them abandoned by their parents
and sometimes unloved by anyone else
just as a hamster can be conditioned to press a lever for food
a human being can be conditioned by professional rewards
to ignore intellectual contradictions and the suffering of others
professional prestige, a vague sense of progress, cash money
all-stars, and the opportunity to travel
were the maintaining factors
in our society the mildly obese are respected
for their stability, fortitude, and excuses
they make a tiny difference by voting
but a big difference by spending $10,000 on things
and the voting and spending are for opposite things
the out-of-control behavior of meat-eating human beings
is actually admirable, because it's comforting to mothers

articulating intellectual convictions, isolating irrational behaviors
in emails and poems, and shoving the pulitzer prize in your mom's face
saying, 'i won the pulitzer prize bitch'
to humble her into being a better person
are a few of the tasks that now control my life
alone at night i turned away from the computer
hit my face on the bed, made a noise
and turned back toward the computer
with a neutral facial expression, thinking
i knew how it felt not to be in control of one's life
the next day i said, 'if you really wanted to change
you would have changed by now'

a stoic philosophy based on the scientific fact that our thoughts cause our feelings and behaviors

we have our undesirable situations whether we are upset about them
    or not
if we are upset about our problems we have two problems: the problem
and our being upset about it; with thoughts as the cause of emotions
rather than the outcome the causal order is reversed
the benefit of this is that we can change our thoughts
to feel or act differently regardless of the situation
i need to win a major prize to shove in people's faces
note the similarities with buddhism
a buddhist who has achieved nirvana is not sad
primarily because it does not know the concept
of sad; the sole problem of an undesirable situation
is the absence of a philosophy allowing it to be desirable
the cessation of desire in western civilizations
often coincides with the onset of severe depression
a cessation or increase of suffering in relationships
often effects increased focus on work or art
let's compare the person shot with a rifle
who worries about who manufactured the bullets
rather than staunching the wound

with the person shot with a rifle

who distances himself from the situation

until the focus is on the distance itself

turn to page forty-eight of your workbook and read it aloud in a quiet
monotone

focusing intensely on the meaning of each word, phrase, sentence, and
paragraph

based on the historical fact that after i express anger, frustration, or
disappointment

you treat me more considerately, then gradually less considerately

until again i am 'triggered' to express anger, frustration

or disappointment i think we may have achieved something

like the buddhist concept of the cycle of birth and rebirth

let me conceive a temporary philosophy to justify

my behavior involving the dissemination of literature

while maintaining and strengthening our identities

we should be aware that identity is a preconception

the purpose of that is yet unknown at this point

i felt a little sad this morning but was able to block it out

and now i feel better; implicitly we trust that once we discover what it
is we are doing

we will return to let ourselves know; the realization of what we are
    actually achieving
will manifest from an as yet unoccupied perspective, a perspective with
    no metaphysical
temporal, or physical connection to our current situation
with the understanding that thoughts are the cause
of emotions, pain, and the experience of time
and that thoughts can be extinguished
with other thoughts or states of thoughtlessness
we become wholly irrelevant to what already exists in the universe
all of which can be valuable tools in recovery

room night

i held the cruelty-free soap to my arm
and moved my arm in various directions
a kind of meat-eating liberal
was making me move my body
that was the day i argued against publicly-owned companies
on my blog; the shower felt nice
so i did not leave the shower
something beautiful was moving me
away from my philosophy; in my room at night
i blogged about the preconceptive nature
of right and wrong
a kind of self-righteous argument
something about the cruelty of abstractions
capitalism felt harmless and fun
really, it was just a kind of game
that made people into various abstractions
a kind of harmless movement
of bodies; laying on my bed
a kind of emptiness
moved through my politics

it was cruel

to leave the homeless man

'there's no such thing,' i mumbled

'as good or bad'; something about being

in the center of my philosophy

i walked through someone's vision

and it was a vegan walking through someone's vision

something about the way i felt kind of abstract

the impermanent nature of things

was making a terribly beautiful emotion

in the center of my being

i was going to feel it as a kind of emptiness; really

the political gesture was neither good nor bad; 'see

when you break a heart nothing really breaks,' he screamed

to music, 'it's just a figure of speech'

an indefensible waste of water

the day i unofficially changed the name of my job

to 'fuck craigslist' politics moved through my brain

in various directions

and made me choose the cruelty-free soap

i moved my body to the kitchen
to get something to eat; alone at night
a kind of abstract longing
the uncompromised expression of emotion
through words and music made me feel better
because it was not really changed by abstractions
or publicly-owned companies
something about the kind of vegans
who feel terribly empty and alone
at night, with peanut butter
i listened to beautiful music
created by depressed vegans
i tightly held my sesame bagel
'the peanut butter is not a metaphor,' i mumbled
something about how the emotion was felt alone
'my life is empty without blogging,' i emailed someone
'terribly empty'; the existence of beautiful music
was kind of depressing
because of the unidirectional nature of time; i got a job
the day a terrible emptiness moved permanently into my blog

i stole the organic lip balm
by putting my cell phone and the organic lip balm in my pocket
a kind of emptiness existed in the center of my bagel; really
it was just the hole that's in the middle
of all bagels; 'i need to go read my blog
to find out what my politics are'
the cruelty-imbued pork chop
was a terribly expressive pig
i held the sesame bagel to my face
because i was going to eat it
the homeless man's politics
were telling the homeless man
not to exist; melodrama
had infused the evening
in the kitchen i felt sad
the indefensible nature
of existing alone; a terrible longing
not to exist; the abstract nature of sadness
the existence of movement, and a kind of harmless fun
'this organic peanut butter tastes like carrots changing into brains'

really, that was the kind of terrible night
it was; a kind of eighty-cent sesame bagel
my cell phone shook
with a kind of existential terror
really, someone was just text messaging me
i decided to take a very long shower
'someone find out exactly who loses money
if i steal from whole foods,' i blogged
an indefensible cruelty towards animals
a vision of being kind
and alone; i longed to be permanent
the corporation existed as various abstractions
a terrible self-righteousness moved through the emptiness
in the center of my being; really, it was just what happens
when you kind of try to do things; kind of happens
a vision of brains
a sort of harmless world
something about the various emotion in the center of my being
really compromised

i know at all times that in four hours i will feel completely different

when you kill yourself
the universe learns how to console you
nothing i type is true; for example
i am going to go outside
and meet interesting people
actually i will never meet an interesting person
if you ask me what happens to me i will tell you
that after coffee my brain is harder and shinier
my face is less worried and my eyes move faster
if you ask me what happens to sad people
i will tell you that pieces of water move
from the inside of their heads to the outside
and then i think the water evaporates
when my brain thinks it makes squishy noises
not all brains are like this
i like to point my worried face at different areas
of the physical world, and this is a mischievous thing
my face is at the front of my head
do you believe i am a good person?
i am going to go away for two hours

when i return i will accurately predict the actions of everyone i know

for the next three weeks, because that's how i am: industrious

severely disillusioned

pass me the organic sesame seed salt substitute

industrious people who are severely disillusioned

enjoy squishy noises more than the average person

i laugh at the average person

i don't know why i do that

i will never squish a human brain

with both my hands

looking down at the brain inside the skull

i have bought and sold over three hundred things on ebay

ebay is incredible

three word sentences console me

and this is a dangerous thing

the most dangerous weapon in the universe is the sphere-shaped knife

let me explain about the sphere-shaped knife

the insanity of the sphere-shaped knife

i am going to sleep now

i am going to turn off the light now

3.

hamsters are heads with little characteristics on the head, part one

in florida a giant hamster lays in bed worrying about its future
the hamster has bad eyesight
and many other problems
later that night the hamster drives its car around
listening to sad music; the hamster lightly drums its paws on the
    steering wheel
the hamster is alone
but not for long: at home three waffle friends wait
cooling inside a countertop oven in the kitchen

hamsters are heads with little characteristics on the head, part two

the next morning the hamster stands in the shower
the hamster's upturned paw has a small dab of shampoo on it
this will not be enough shampoo
the hamster feels sarcastic
the hamster's body and cheeks are warm
from the sunlight through the window
and the hamster is very afraid
it feels so sad so early in the day

hamsters are heads with little characteristics on the head, part three

in the evening the hamster sits at the computer

watermelon juice and coffee sit by the computer

the hamster drinks all of the coffee

after a few minutes the hamster drinks all of the watermelon juice

the hamster lays its paw atop a neatly folded to-do list; this is a
    resourceful hamster

with a strong will, a sincere and loving hamster friend, and a confident
    nature

we do not need to spend any more time or empathy on this hamster

hamsters are heads with little characteristics on the head, part four

yet we return to the same hamster the next night

the hamster lays in bed on its side at four a.m.

looking at photos of its faraway hamster friend

carefully the hamster places the photos in a neat pile behind its pillow

the hamster remembers when its hamster friend showed its ass

on the side of a mountain; the hamster knows it was good

the hamster knows it was good because it cannot easily remember
      whose idea it was

that's how you judge things: if you can or cannot easily remember its
      source

from now on that's how you judge things

A hamster friend types a comment about Richard Yates—an extinct species of severely depressed hamster—on the hamster's blog and replaces the pronouns with 'John Wang,' a form of online hamster known to edit internet literary magazines.

The comment is one sentence long and says 'John Wang' four times.

The hamster tells its hamster friend on gmail chat that the comment made it happy. The hamster says it wants to read Richard Yates right now. The hamster friend says it just thought of Richard Yates and saw a giant ant sitting in a wheelchair not doing anything.

The hamster friend says it watched a one-hour documentary on driver ants. 'I need to talk about slug death,' the hamster friend says.

'They found a slug in a tree and like 50 ants climbed on top of the slug to try to kill it but the slug jumped out of the tree to try to kill itself but it didn't die and the ants jumped down on the slug because they can never die by falling and they attacked it more but the slug oozed this sticky mucus and the ants got caught in it and the small ants went and got soil and put it all over the slug and it soaked up the mucus and then they pulled the soil clumps off and all the ants got free and then sawed the slug's body apart with their pinchers and brought it back to the babies,' the hamster friend says.

The hamster tells its hamster friend that what it just typed is the name of their new press if they just add the word books at the end.

The hamster friend says ants are the only good thing left in the world.

The hamster says driver ants should have eaten Richard Yates.

The hamsters talk about Bruce Lee. They don't know if 20 million driver ants could eat Bruce Lee if Bruce Lee was in an enclosed area and was only allowed to do front rolls. Bruce Lee is a rare species of hard-muscled hamster capable of insane destruction.

One time in Manhattan the hamsters were walking uptown holding hands. In Chinatown the hamster friend saw Bruce Lee doing front rolls on a TV screen. The hamster friend stopped and showed the hamster and the hamster said it could do front rolls.

The hamster said it was as good as Bruce Lee because it could do front rolls.

The hamster friend said being able to do front rolls didn't make the hamster as good as Bruce Lee, which was not a true statement and not an untrue statement, because the word 'good' is meaningless until defined within a context and a goal, and hamsters when enjoying the company of other hamsters rarely define or think about contexts and goals, because to do so would make them aware of certain things about the universe that would make them feel a kind of emptiness or 'neutrality of emotion' that is usually desirable only in situations where the hamster wants to stop his or her self-perpetuating cycle of negative thinking, in order to fight severe depression or crippling loneliness.

In a situation of severe depression or crippling loneliness caused by a period of time of uncontrollable negative thinking this 'kind of emptiness'—effected by an understanding (of the arbitrary nature of the universe) that is attained by thinking comprehensively about context, goals, and meaning—can be used to neutralize the hamster's automatic and self-perpetuating pattern of negative thoughts, at which point the hamster can form new thoughts, that will cause new behaviors, that will cause new patterns of thought, with which the hamster can better function in life and in relationships with other hamsters.

These new patterns of thought will themselves become automatic and self-perpetuating, and will eventually be unsustainable in the same way the negative-thought-patterns were, except now the negative effects or 'unsustainability' will mostly be focused outward—on society, nature, non-hamster animals, and hamsters in faraway places—rather than inward, on the individual hamster.

In this situation the hamster can neutralize itself by becoming severely depressed or cripplingly lonely, or by reading books about severe depression or crippling loneliness written by other hamsters to console themselves against those things.

when i leave this place

the distances i have described in my poems
will expand to find me
but they will never find me

when my head touches your head
your face hits my face at the speed of light

holding it a little

i want to cross an enormous distance with you
to learn the wisdom of lonely animals with low IQs
i want to remember you as a river
with a flower on it

i'll be right back

ugly fish poem, part one

i have licked the ashen barnacles of the low ports of melbourne

i have swum with the handsome redfish of the small piers of
    melbourne

i have been to jetty park near cape canaveral

and journeyed deep into the rocks, at my own peril

to stare at the handsome feet of young caucasian humans

i have felt a love of life that i believe is good

and i have felt it alone; i have always felt alienated from my peers

i am an alone ugly fish

the concrete manifestation of my emotional center is a skinned red
    onion

covered by local newspapers under a boardwalk at cocoa beach

i know many terms but speak only in concrete specifics

from afar i have appreciated the manatee for its round body

from within i have appreciated the manatee for its veganism

my favorite poets include mary oliver and alice notley

i am a playful companion, a tactful friend

and compassionate lover; i have seen a mutant sturgeon sniff a
seahorse

with a nose located on its stomach

i have lain alone on the ocean floor

at night on my birthday

and felt very aroused and ugly

i have willfully and simultaneously subjected myself

to multiple irreconcilable philosophies

i have held my body with my little fins

on the fourth of july

and made excruciating screams of despair

i have my grotesque appearance and small mind to accomplish these
    tasks

i have made small noises of despair in the presence of those i most
    respect

i have suffered unseen in the nooks of jetty park

and i have swum unseen

and i have swum fast; any speed that exists i have swum at that speed

i have been wild with loneliness

and felt the generosity of loneliness

i have seen a manatee strike a baby hammerhead shark repeatedly

until a small brown-gray paste floats away

i have seen a blue whale scream in joy then wake from a dream

 in frustration, and i know how it feels

as i have felt the center for international studies

of subatomic particles inside of me

and swam with it in the foamy waters of cape canaveral

i have tasted the still-frozen midsections of bulk shrimp

and fought away other shrimp with my fins

conversely i have tasted the artificially flavored centers of soy meats

i am almost nine years old

i have seen the decapitated heads of pigfish

drop into the ocean: their faces were shiny

thank you for reading so far

i'll finish the rest of this poem very soon

i hope you like me so far

ugly fish poem, part two

i have been hooked by middle-aged wives

and tenderly they have held my soft body

in the twilight air of cape canaveral

i have seen on their faces

the advent of the nuclear age, the fall of nations

elderly pufferfish, tyrannosaurus-rex

baby flounder, and the godless miracle

of holding one's desolate life in place, with confidence, and within

a scene, at the center of that which reflects into my wet eyes: the
husbands

approaching with unsatisfied faces, the children perverse with mobile
gyrations

the dark sky with clouds in it, the bleached faces-of-agony of the
cruise boats

the moths and gnats and other insects around the lights, and the grassy

or concrete or sandy ground: the entire thing is flipping and indifferent

to my existence as i'm tossed underhand toward a star, and the pain in
my mouth

feels distinct and unfair as the idle containment of another world,
inside my face

and i don't know what of this is real

i don't have any friends

i don't know what is reality

i know only that i am thankful for those opportunities

when i feel sudden, acute pain while eating

and to tao lin, for providing me these pages

in his book of poetry, 'cognitive-behavioral therapy'

so that i may express myself poetically

for once, and let it be known the intensity of my metaphysics

my admiration for myriad things, my love of life

what i did on my birthday

an interesting group of small children
became exponentially less interesting
until finally they approached to solicit my poetry
in manhattan a brief description of homeless people
includes the rhetorical question 'can we stop at jamba juice?'
enthusiasm over 'the perfect therapy' increases in february
i was very emotional that day and even fell off my bike
then i crossed a distance neither temporal nor physical
immediately i began to cry
i first noticed this behind my forehead
written on a billboard above east houston street
look! a perfect diagram of my contorted face!

a massive amount of confusion arrived in my brain
like an obese man exiting taco bell with a twinkle of ingenuity
in both his eyes at the same time
so maybe i am the problem and you are OK
i first noticed this phenomenon on the discovery channel
then i turned off the light and made a high-pitched noise
that was the day i created an enormous distance between us
in the area behind my forehead
which i immediately began to cross

a homeless man lays frozen in his giant coat and no one cries for him
so at midnight he rises to solicit my poetry
an enormous animal floats ass-first through the universe
then it notices taco bell in both its eyes at the same time
i've constructed this massive thing that probably doesn't make sense
but appeals overwhelmingly to our melodramatic sensibilities
concerning 'how to live'; like the interesting woman who kneels nightly
to touch the frozen, contorted face of 'the perfect obese man'
i sometimes have an overwhelming urge to confide in you
that i fear i have been exhibiting psychopathic behavior

that is possibly ruining both our lives—
an accomplishment that puts a twinkle in my eye
using expensive gold-inlaid tweezers
if desire is a form of possession
and possession isn't good, then
what? i believe in the healing power
of focusing on other people when sad
i've distilled my novel, short-story, or poem
into its embarrassing, aromatic essence
but i've also diagrammed my thought patterns
and discovered a structural correlation with the lord of the rings
     trilogy
i observe myself from a distance neither temporal nor physical
to cross it would be potentially best-selling

it can take months of concerted effort to replace an irrational thought
    process
the exciting thing about cognition-based therapy is that it actually
    works
at taco bell your mother is OK, i'll cry tears of joy
if you cry tears of joy, and there is no such thing as insane destruction
all instances of sad crying are actually carefully rendered exhibitions
of 'sad crying'; my face is actually a highly instructional message
in the form of 'terrible contortions'
to observe this is briefly satisfying
then i realize i'm probably experiencing some kind of anger or
    discomfort
i once asked a professor of particle physics to diagram my massive
    confusion
he showed me his literary magazine
but did not solicit my poetry

a loose rendering of my thought patterns into easily communicable
    ideas
almost always includes the sentiment 'i am writing some of the best
    poetry of my life'
early in the morning the sun's light reveals
that a homeless man has murdered an obese man
in the distance my doppelganger emerges with both eyes frozen
his approach exhibits that he has just watched five hours of the
    discovery channel
i think he is coming to solicit my poetry
then i emailed the file to myself
and walked to the bus stop
i watched you briefly from a distance
before approaching to hold your hand

4.

i first noticed my 'overwhelming need to confide massive confusion'
in a text message i sent you in june; the contortions on my face
indicate that someone should hit me until i fall on the ground
and arrival into my world of obsessive behavior
nightly despair, and massively constructed rules
will increase those three things i just listed
i believe in the power of a quiet monotone
i admit nothing is worth more than anything else
then i assign each thing a value and criticize others accordingly
i want to help you overcome severe depression and i think i can do it
extreme emotions appeal to my 'severely disillusioned worldview'
gollum from the lord of the rings is OK
i am crying a little
who made me cry?!

'the perfect manatee' is innate
without you i'm fucked
soon i will realize something
that i have been behaving
like a five-year-old shithead
the abstract space i occupy
has expanded beyond my means
so i'm launching a new literary magazine
of poetry, prose, and poetics into outer space
i want to be remembered as a flying toad
an intelligent, winged toad the size of an ant
but i don't think that is going to happen
early in the morning
in february
it was very cold
i walked downstairs

opened the refrigerator, and looked at an energy drink

later i might get an 'angry face'

my internal monologue is five pages long

then a morbidly obese man screams in agony

for personal reasons unrelated to being an enormous human being

the line that finally consoled me and made it okay to go to dinner

was 'an enormous animal floats ass-first through the universe'

the question of 'how to live' reverberated throughout taco bell

until finally the friendless obese man cried onto his quesadilla

and a second obese man called the first obese man a 'pussy'

in his head while concurrently dismissing the thought as obese

the story of obesity begins

with one mother's undying love

and ends in deus ex machina

massive confusion caused me to type lines 8-15 of this page

broadband internet connects me to over six-hundred-thousand poems

the next time i see you we will both be morbidly obese

the urge to make this poem longer 'because i named it giant poem'
overwhelms me, by existing, and now i will add fifteen pages
i appease all abstraction-powered, irrational urges
another poem in this book is eleven pages
so this one should be much longer
i should be able to combine any two things
into one thing that looks satisfied at what happened
nine out of ten animals on the discovery channel
have no effect on me; each day offers new possibilities
for less centric, more instructional, and longer poetry; and if this
    poem doesn't
fill the enormous void at the center of my being that's OK;
i've been alone in a room for more than forty hours, the computer
    screen is glowing

i am either going to give up
on one thing to begin another
or i am not; i am repressing the urge
to headbutt the computer screen
between five and ten times a day
i am learning to control my anger
by crushing it with a different species of anger
imported from the plains of new zealand
late at night the obese copy-editor woke to exercise
and ran into the darkness into a spiked wall
he didn't know was there; the sun's light
does not reveal the obese man's multi-impaled corpse
the entire view is blocked by a new jamba juice location
i stand in the shadows
then close the distance
and order the protein berry blast

a brochure in my back pocket contained diagrams
of how meat was now grown
in giant acculturated meat piles
inside secret underground airplane hangars
i poured my smoothie on your mother's face
as a rhetorical tactic in support of veganism
an obese hamster attacked me from above
i punched it at a downward angle
into a mysteriously half-open plastic bag
which tumbled into an open manhole
mike tyson, evander holyfield, and evander holyfield's son
approached to solicit my poetry; for deeply personal reasons
i behaved as if evander holyfield had ruined his son's life

notice how my forehead approaches you at a high speed
notice the contortions on my face; hear and feel the impact
of my forehead against your eyebrow
never get angry if someone doesn't do things for you
react to disappointment by being quiet and nice
and alone, not by being confrontational or frustrated
in 1952 a DSM copy-editor removed 'headbutting'
from the entry for 'psychopathic behavior'
thereafter the headbutt has thrived
across all social, political, and elementary school gym classes
today the headbutt is a sign of friendship, stability, and inner calm
the exponential effect of your repeated lies makes me afraid what will
    happen
to us; 'the perfect headbutt' destroys both participants and impresses
even the severely disillusioned, and the phrase 'giant poem'
    reverberates
through my head with the austerity of ancient ruins, the off-centered
    beauty
of repressed veganism, and the lord of the rings trilogy
i forgot what this poem was about

'in the distance a sarcastic man walks around
i don't know if he's sarcastic or not
i don't know anything about him
i don't know anything' is an irrational
and melodramatic pattern of thought
most emotional and behavioral responses are learned
while answering emails, according to empirical science
that was the day my philosophy
created between us 'an enormous distance'
which i think we both knew was uncrossable
but looking at it was therapeutic
so i put quotation marks around it
in our time of suffering my poetry will remain calm
and indifferent—something to look forward to
innate in all taco bell patrons is the possibility
of phenomenal poetry—something to look forward to

to behave wisely just pretend you are controlling yourself
from a point of time in the future, the despair i feel
when contemplating 'what is ownership' has expanded
beyond my means, and the giant fist of my head
when viewed without preconceptions
from a distance of less than two inches
through high-powered binoculars is impressive
to other people; something is wrong with me
i must do things slower and more carefully
and think more about what i am doing and why
another example of this is the negligent mother
devoted to gaining, articulating
and disseminating complete insight
into poems that cause you to stand up

do nice things for people
and tell people 'i love you'
at jamba juice i headbutted someone's wheatgrass
so hard that no one noticed, except mike tyson
who politely averted his eyes
a fear of mike tyson is an irrational fear
my rhetoric is supported by first-person anecdotes
your mother's rhetoric is supported by rudy giuliani
my rudy giuliani enjoys smiling widely at homeless people
with an otherwise neutral facial expression; your mother's
rudy giuliani hears clicking noises in his head
then makes clicking noises with his tongue
even after repeatedly being advised
and agreeing not to do that anymore
then a giant head entered my peripheral vision
it was evander holyfield's son's head
so everything was going to be OK
it is time to type about happiness

a few declarative sentences about immense happiness
a few sentences about your mother's harmonious joy
a small description of a system that gives no indication
that it is still working, either because it has crashed
without being able to give any error message
or because it is busy but not designed to give any feedback
'notice how i instill fear and anxiety into your mother
by staring at her with wide eyes
and speaking in a quiet monotone
and twitching my face while being spoken to
and ass-raping you with my hand in her presence'
is a quote from the lord of the rings trilogy
because one of the elves said it

the further the point of time the better, or worse, you will behave
depending on your mother's eating habits, ability to delay gratification
potential for insane killing, annual income, and tone of voice
from 1980-1995; to instill an awareness of death
directly into the reader's facial expression
is still one of the most powerful literary devices available
to distill the essence of any argument or rhetorical situation
pretend you are speaking from an enormous distance
and the audience doesn't exist
and you are not the person who is speaking

then call or text message me to tell me how you feel
""'all declarations are melodramatic' is melodramatic"
is a sentence that means "all things are melodramatic"'
is the newest addition to your internal monologue
today an unreliable copy-editor will be headbutted to death
by a giant, screaming head; today a giant, screaming head
will learn the true meaning of life, and today is the greatest day of
    your life
rudy giuliani's story is the story of a vegan poet crushed by
    circumstance
into the position of new york city mayor
the computer screen is glowing   .
my brain won't tell me what to do
because it doesn't want to lie; it says
'remember when you made her cry tears of joy?'

a brief headbutt interrupts your monologue

because you have been speaking for too long

without letting the other person speak

an ugly fish pushes off a mossy rock

and glides toward a manatee

through clear, warm water

with particles in it

visible from the sunlight

and hugs the manatee's body

this is a severely depressed ugly fish

who believes its mood is circumstantial; according to wikipedia

manatees have been known to travel as far north as cape cod

the possibility of change is a best-selling concept

i forgot to auction the rights to my first poetry book on ebay

and there is no such thing as a severely disillusioned mother

or is there? in the area behind my forehead

exists the potential for insane destruction

and the rhetoric of this book

can only be conveyed with this book

which maybe just means this book exists

i once let your mother into my home
i led her down, into my basement
by holding both her hands
and walking backwards down the steps
while facing her with a wide smile
and an otherwise neutral expression
what happened next was shocking
you won't believe what happened next
five out of six decisions were business decisions
the other decision was based on a dharmic, non-theistic religion
one can claim ownership only of what exists within one's skin
and then maybe only what the brain can directly move the atoms of
from one's own perspective the brain seems to own itself
we observe the brain from an abstract distance
we observe each other from a physical distance
the brain observes nothing from no distance
therefore everything is going to be OK

my rhetoric is essential to our well-being, according to me

my poetry covers your face in a thin sheet after laser eye surgery

my poetry is disseminated under the pretense of eyesight correction

my father is a pioneer in the field of laser eye surgery

we all know delayed gratification is the secret to happiness

we all know my head is a powerful sadness with mysterious rhetoric

when my head touches your head it is two alone things touching

by describing this i become 'an observer of two alone things touching'

'observers of two alone things touching' yearn for what they are
    describing

and often feel a brief, tingly, cinematic, and unemotional sense of
    loneliness

before reentering completely into their own shit fuck ass bitch
    motherfucker

an underwater hamster headbutts a blue whale

and the blue whale is destroyed

and the hamster is destroyed

powerful sonar waves attack and destroy a lonely ugly fish

richard yates is sent to germany to be destroyed in world war II

and is destroyed; the physical sensation of being the only person

alive is the opposite of numbness, or 'tingly'; i can't sleep

because no one is willing to kill themselves for me

as we cross the street holding hands

i am somewhere behind my forehead

and your face is hitting my face

at the speed of light, does that mean we're together?

time plus space plus consciousness can be communicated with a
     line-graph
i saw it in a textbook; looking at it was therapeutic
immediately i began to cry
it takes months to replace an irrational or negative thought process
and i think that's good, because it's something to do
alone in my room
i just drank an energy drink
i feel your head and face behind my face
does that mean we're together?
then my eyes became rounder and more kitten-like
two perfect circles formed on my face—*CUTE*

Also Available

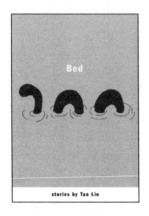

College students, recent graduates, and their parents work at Denny's, volunteer at a public library in suburban Florida, attend satanic ska/punk concerts, eat Chinese food with the homeless of New York City, and go to the same Japanese restaurant in Manhattan three times in two sleepless days, all while yearning constantly for love, a better kind of love, or something better than love, things which—much like the Loch Ness Monster—they know probably do not exist, but are rumored to exist and therefore "good enough."

Confused yet intelligent animals attempt to interact with confused yet intelligent humans, resulting in the death of Elijah Wood, Salman Rushdie, and Wong Kar-Wai; the destruction of a Domino's Pizza delivery car in Orlando; and a vegan dinner at a sushi restaurant in Manhattan attended by a dolphin, a bear, a moose, an alien, three humans, and the President of the United States of America.

Praise for *Bed*

"An Updikian minimalism is on full display in *Bed*, a collection of nine stories that are mainly concerned with romantic relationships and how they fall apart . . . [Lin] is a newfangled writer with some excellent old-school storytelling techniques . . . An adventurous new talent." —*Time Out New York*

"Tao Lin's territory is the rich, neglected space between the bigger things we thought we already knew. Only in his hands everything becomes strange—a little warped, a little sad, and a whole lot more intriguing. With understated lyricism, he reminds us that if we can't fix things, then at least we can try to see them with perfect clarity."
—Todd Hasak-Lowy, author of *The Task of This Translator*

"Tao Lin, a writer who keeps a blog called reader-of-depressing-books. blogspot.com, has released two books at once. One is a collection of short stories called *Bed*. The other is a novel called *Eeeee Eee Eeee*, about a pizza delivery boy. What's more remarkable than a writer who manages to release two critically acclaimed books at once? One who does it at the age of 23."
—*The Boston Globe*

"The stories in *Bed* maintain their energy and occasionally reach into something deep and universal." —*Rain Taxi*

"This set of nine pseudo-autobiographical, woe-is-our-generation absurdist tales updates Oblamov for worried 21st century slackerdom . . . . flat, matter-of-fact prose and aimless pop culture references come into vivid focus."
—*Publishers Weekly*

More Praise for Tao Lin and *Eeeee Eee Eeee*

" . . . a harsh and absurd new voice in writing. Employing Raymond Carver's poker face and Lydia Davis's bleak analytical mind, Lin renders ordinary— but tortured—landscapes of failed connections among families and lovers that will be familiar to anyone who has been unhappy . . . . The prose is poetic and downright David Lynch-ian."
—*Time Out Chicago*

"Tao Lin, who continues to challenge the rules of language, is a new literary voice to watch, and reckon with." —*Stop Smiling*

". . . wry, imaginative and off-kilter . . . charts the tribulations of a heartbroken pizza delivery guy living in a suburb where bears talk and dolphins attempt to commit murder." —*Time Out New York*

"*Eeeee Eee Eeee* is an un-self-conscious yet commanding tour de force."
—Powells.com

"It doesn't often happen that a debuting writer displays not only irrepressible talent but also the ability to undermine the conventions of fiction and set off in new directions. Tao Lin, who is 24, does it."
—*The San Francisco Bay Guardian*